Storage Shed

Storage Shed

RICH MURPHY

RESOURCE *Publications* · Eugene, Oregon

STORAGE SHED

Copyright © 2025 Rich Murphy. All rights reserved. Except for brief quotations in critical publications or reviews, no part of this book may be reproduced in any manner without prior written permission from the publisher. Write: Permissions, Wipf and Stock Publishers, 199 W. 8th Ave., Suite 3, Eugene, OR 97401.

Resource Publications
An Imprint of Wipf and Stock Publishers
199 W. 8th Ave., Suite 3
Eugene, OR 97401

www.wipfandstock.com

PAPERBACK ISBN: 979-8-3852-4944-2
HARDCOVER ISBN: 979-8-3852-4945-9
EBOOK ISBN: 979-8-3852-4946-6

VERSION NUMBER 04/29/25

For Bonnie Martin

"Art is only a means to life, to the life more abundant. It is not in itself the life more abundant. It merely points the way, something which is overlooked not only by the public, but very often by the artist himself. In becoming an end; it defeats itself."

—Henry Miller

Contents

Acknowledgments | xi

Pots and Slate
The Who | 3
Dinghy | 4
Spine Sprinkler | 5
Innocence Agenda | 6
The Nose for Life | 7
Wink (an exercise) | 8
Umbilical Dimple | 9
Fetish Features | 10
Modern Author | 11
Will Well Mine | 12
Dory Speak | 13
In the Way | 14
The Mole Toll | 15
Fear Factor | 16
Falling | 17
Dennis Menace | 18
Sci-Fi Ambience | 19
"Welcome Mat!" | 20
Silver Platters | 21
Protocol for a Parable | 22
The Banality Drama | 23
Hero | 24

Tools

Cranium Terrarium | 27
Cave Dwelling | 28
Hypnopompia | 29
Hypnagogia | 30
Ethic Op Props | 31
Geologist Pick | 33
Whinny Wear | 34
The Infiltrated State | 35
Anatomic Passion | 37
Common Senses | 38
Dear Great Grandchildren, | 39
Fiction Friction | 40
Argh and then Argot and Matey | 41
Speech Act Moment | 42
Ouch, All Together | 43
Dogged | 44
Asteroid Nations | 45
Banality Bulbs | 46
The Fix | 47
Marshland Rag | 48
Lifeboat | 49
The Catch | 50

The Stash

Slug Mug | 53
That Mean Mirth | 54
Dressing Despair | 55
In the Morass | 56
Milk in the Newspapers | 57
Neighbor Relations | 58
Modern Justice | 59
Fabric Fault | 60
Diatribal Tangent | 61
Cities' Limits | 63
The Prime Prevention | 64

Tongues | 65
Game | 66
Twenty-four Hours News Channel | 67
The Surprise Parties | 68
Habitual Habitat | 69
Story Lines | 70
Behind the Lines | 71
Denial Bile | 72
In Skin Sin | 73
For the Ride | 74
The Drive | 75

Garden Expeditions

Isolation Station | 79
Home on the Range | 80
Facing the Many Small Bangs | 81
Bungle Bundle | 82
Self-Help Medium | 83
Off the Grid | 84
The Motorway | 85
Moving Fixtures | 86
Knock Knock | 87
Roadmap | 88
Grumble, Grouse, Teehee | 89
Invisible Ink | 90
History's Empty Nursery | 91
Sewing Machine | 92
On Deck | 93
Fair Thee Well | 94
Todestrieb and the Parasite | 95
The Storage Shed | 96

Acknowledgments

Otoliths—"Dinghy"

Epiphany—"The Nose for Life"

Yes- Poetry—"That Mean Mirth"

The View From Here—"Moving Fixtures"

Eudaimonia—"Milk in Newspaper"

Gloom Cupboard—"The Motorway"

Phati'tude Literary Magazine—"Innocence Agenda"

Fact-Simile—"Ethic Op Props"

Big Bridge—"Cranium Terrarium," "Dear Great Grandchildren"

Silenced Press—"Denial Bile"

Counter-Example—"Dennis Menace"

Spiral Bridge—"The Surprise Party"

Forty Ounce Bachelors—"Portal Properties"

Fjord Review—"Dogged"

The Eloquent Atheist—"Neighbor Relations," "Protocol for a Parable," and "Cities' Limits"

Straitjackets—"Habitual Habitat"

Miracle—"Invisible Ink"

Blast Furnace—"The Catch"

Carnival—"Hypnopompia," "Hypnagogia"

Wild Quarterly—"The Fix" and "Fabric Fault"

Assonance Quarterly—"Dory Speak"

Brev Spread Magazine—"Sewing Machine"

Poydras Review—"In the Morass"

Synesthesia Literary Journal—"Modern Author"

Former People—"Todestrieb and the Parasite"

Backlash Journal—"Lifeboat"

Eunoia Review—"Google Drive"

MadHat Lit—"Will Well Mine" and "Off the Grid"

BlazeVox Movies—"Silver Platters"

Futures Trading—"Isolation Station"

West Texas Review—"Cave Dwelling"

Pots and Slate

"...we maintain religious/cultural/political shams to hold our self-perception intact, much in the same way that the lunatic believes he is telling the truth, or in the way we continue to lie even when we suddenly remember that we are wrong and the person we argue with is correct."
—Slavoj Zizek

"...already the animals are aware
that we are not at home in
our interpreted world."
—Rainer Maria Rilke

"Fragments of a vessel which are to be glued together must match one another in the smallest details, although they need not be like one another. In the same way a translation, instead of resembling the meaning of the original, must lovingly and in detail incorporate the original's mode of signification, thus making both the original and the translation recognizable as fragments of a greater language, just as fragments are part of a vessel."
—Walter Benjamin, Illuminations:
  Essays and Reflections

The Who

"Who are you, who who, who who?"
—The Who

Pushing and pulling into character
the stranger waking beside each spouse,

the mirror fraud pieces together
for a kitchen and door

Cardboard cut outs hold at some point
where a conversation promises

Authentic tall-tales voice to harmonize
or counterpoint

A calendar and wild imagination
fold along perforations galore
and in old age pastes for children

Presence presents on subversive stages
morning, noon, and night:

Ta da, ta da, ta da desires to embrace
each freak instant, each fear-filled accident

A news report wrestles with the reader:

Label guns kill for fun;
otherwise Who, on first, eats

Dinghy

Emptying from consciousness
the deep blue sea, the bailer
hoped someday to know
a bucket, a boat, a continent.
Instead, the drifter in a lather
learns with other psyche sailors
sound waves: a bucket, a boat,
countenance. A tongue slips
on wet surfaces gagging meaning.
A god would laugh.
SOS abbreviates help
further from coastlines.
Any fisherman baits the quiet
for sanity and desires surface.
The lifeboat promises little
to the swimmer swallowing.
Hollowed out speech
strapped to breath acts,
a kind sail or flapping gull.
John Donne must never have
woken to his treading water.
The stars Odysseus left
in the sky require oars.
Between nine-tenths
submerged intentions
and Plymouth Mock,
small craft takes on the world.

Spine Sprinkler

Even from the manicured dawns
and within pruned, herbicidal
evenings, courage takes root.
How does mettle flourish
within schools that graduate
jellyfish? The well-watered
suburban livers would seem
to fail at backbone near a lawn.
Perhaps because nail file, clipper,
and sprays mow down a business
foe, grubs, and crab grass
don't stand. If the briefcase carries,
breakfast serial behavior must
knead tool shed trolls into stuffed
animals to control, restrain,
and lay puppies awake near bedrooms
for children. Irritants in a shell
refine necks. However, now
and then grit on a welcome mat
grows to oak and the right hand
that rose holds firm a promise.

Innocence Agenda

Embedded in behavior, belief taunts
tongues pointing out concerns and generosity.
Stories lead listeners to the primroses
while forty, sixty, eighty hours tromp and trump.
The mirror has everything backwards.
Daily, someone else receives the close shave.
Any reflection has the dweller
smiling ear to ear: Hounds sound far off.
What trail has been covered?
While a stalker reads these words,
more polemics have been written,
and one alibi trips over two perpetrators.

The Nose for Life

The iceberg on shoulders celebrates
a reputation for what seems apparent
but could tear a whole in a hold
or doom a polar bear to a cold
drink around a backyard swimming pool.
Most often, unseen remains unreal,
adrift confusion, impressions, motivations
from instinct and intuition.
The background poise speaks volume
about the tip and acts on the cool sailor
or third-class passenger. The dog wags a tale.
The sliver shiver on occasion
recognizes the evening sky
harboring the universe up a sleeve.

Wink (an exercise)

A Swiss army mask
rests in amniotic fluid.
The showcase bulges,
rumbles, and thumps.
When purchased,
new features for every mood express.
A personality never needs
to pose or dispose. Bank on it!
The cash register rings
and a creature creeps
from a womb with a mug and arms.
Semi-sweets and cigars
gush over the top. Watch.
Doctors and nurses
hold back horror with a smile:
(Don't come too close).

Umbilical Dimple

The public relations officer
assumes all Is own eyes pasted
to the center of the universe.
Undivided attention from holes
in heads onto the first and last button
on one birthday suit propagates
a good fortune. However, each navel
absorbs a self that sponge-bathes
oblivious in the obvious. The sun
revolves around every knot
worshipper each moment on Earth.
Humility spins in other galaxies perhaps.
The marketing schemes brand
the steer for the store and chute,
the avoider-patient for the big day.
Contests to describe to the Poseidon
school the interior to the fishbowl
corral shrimps for comparison before
the ice, sauce, and the swallow.
Dear clients mis-speak before breaking,
gas bubbles on the surface.

Fetish Features

Beneath the social gesture,
a citizen knows different.
The wave either way distracts
community from real concern.
The symbol among so many fingers
or thoughts dancing around some
irritating object define the terms
in any debate. Reasoning may
become sidetracked
to protocol or pathos but fixation
brings the trifle back to a point.
Any obligation to family or fiends
annoys the riveted robot until
the fascination captures a mind.
The matter haunts the interaction
should an arbiter study the vital signs:
Disorder grips mobs with "excuse me."

Modern Author

Installed in the air-conditioned
nightmare, the autobiography
presents a hero who freezes
awaiting the back cover.
Ancestors built houses using
symbols available from the dead.
Today, the box owner maintains
the windowless prison cell
when so much emptiness invites
creativity. While alternative noons
pass outside the metaphor regime,
the comfort convict celebrates
with nightlights and police patrols.
The ghost prompts Panic Stricken
in the vibrating electric chair
each morning and the evening
constructs an abominable snowman
that digs a grave in the front yard.
For the reader in lockdown
any wooing sends a mate through
thin ice before the epilogue.

Will Well Mine

Seldom does talent dam tear ducts,
cement nostrils using mucus,
or avoid a cleaning under fingernails.
Aptitude inspires filing nails but never
to the quick after a good polishing
encourages a bored brow to try
something else, hungers for the grits
that American hardship shovels
under noses, leaving glove marks
across cheeks. In the long run, grit
molests empty wallets into faces
with smiles. In a bedroom, guts
whip into shape every sad sack
lumped among wind-up failures
and balloons with batteries
not included. Fiasco frescos throw
up the uninitiated hands when lemons
bubble from a wall or turkeys flap.
The patient never gets any better.
This race roots for a root.
Pluck stands Puck tall at the podium
and no one notices animal instincts
stuck to a heel, long but perforated.

Dory Speak

When thrown overboard, water wings
don't drop into the harbor
and lodge in the mud at the bottom.
Lungs inflate a moan or argh,
while ears float on the current.
Even Shakespeare must have known:
At best a life vest at the deep end
in a public pool, at worst,
a rubber duck in bathwater.
The bundled letters, written with love,
capture imaginations but "whether" tosses
an idea around in a teacup.
What weight in ink, paper, pixels
requires lead and a bay?
Stringing holds for children singing
perhaps, but links are lost in the chain
reaction and adults slave over absence.
A survivor needs to know
the dog paddle or how to puff at syllables
while getting the drift to things.
Stones may plop, should the bailer
wish to interpret so.

In the Way

The by-stander wades to the neck
through background and fore without emerging
along a shoreline. Walking on water
would bring surer innocence to a witness.
Birds may seem to get over trees,
but the sky boxes bouts if the bill comes due.
The horizon disappeared among eggshells
into a not so kind multilingual discussion.
A peep interferes with experiments,
and a sniff from the sidelines
interrupts everyday practices.
In fact, roots lead to senses
(instigating or reacting)
where virgin forest may have gone
about a certain business as usual.
Results would have turned wood contrary
to the stool leg or banister perhaps.
The frame coddled the ancients
around adolescence with crutches
and excuses, but now the wise creature
holds breath for the universe.
Listening for aum distracts a way.

The Mole Toll

Testing lessons learned, language
whacks any hole that sunk
between a mouth and pencil in the classroom.

The patient graduates bruised,
convinced the hidden has been exposed
to the knees. Diaries flap their covers
to the honey in ears that shine and wink.
Dark and dirty confession bestows
honorary awareness that cleanses
the bestselling rumor-mills.

Judges and religious officials
in every literate home buy vomit
on paper to achieve greater power;
the senseless gorges stand on shoulders.

Even graffiti vandals purge
from pressurized cans 'dreams'
and so just mist commuter conversations.

The life-long-teaching moves restless
at the headboard and in the living room
between the workplace and home.
The more dictionaries consulted,
the more articulate the chasm complexes
and the more vented passages
into a bio-graphical chemistry.

A simple couch crouches in response
to the most sophisticated phrase
that a last breath will ever utter or pen in.

Fear Factor

Though plans catch on contingency,
in generals exit strategies prevail
once a map unfolds: Old age
and history books carry the corpse.
Children often present arms and a device
for dreaming about presence
and absence down the road.
So citizens also study the creases
in topography as the wrinkles pass into
past, or at least the pedestrian may do so.
By feeling around for inspiration
and from possibility pushing and pulling
tools for momentum, a bystander
should not be found. Yet purpose
and tomorrow with few raw materials
petrify miners stretched out in morning
waiting for embalmment.
Buried before engagement while torsos
occupy space, the feet within weather
require choreographers and crutches.
Poets stand the chances
but will never reach the audience
who most often rhymes with bard.

Falling

The saints frisked friction for grace.
Gravity ruled on high even then and there.
Messengers falling into hands suffered
molesters who desired a pinch from dignity.
The thugs felt a need for moon beams
and for the talent for giving up when
lying down. "Arms out to the sides
and spread 'em, angel!" said Ms Snow
to the child-like postal worker.
A slip from adolescence into love
greets with discomfort.

Today, a sincerity pulls down
at the corners on mouths.
While many celebrants throw victory
out the window with the confetti,
others stoop with a dustpan.
The person with the lab coat
focuses on the drag that doesn't
permit eloquence, as joints
and memories buckle one at a time.
All parties inhale foam
and the springs that cushion
year-after-year with unconscious air.
The murmur from the members
farther back in the line empty
humor from nervous pockets.
Sweaty palms applaud for nothing
that lasts from each lifetime achievement.

Dennis Menace

Before the alien bursts through the rib cage
to greet the world, a wolf or bear
escapes through or prowls a forest.

After a stranger pokes a head above bi-ped shoulders,
humans from town and country breathe easier
and welcome the newcomer to a table.

Between the wild and the caesarean section
performed from inside, the death match contestants
negotiate the birth and new born.

Guilt pummels the groin,
and longing kicks the stuffing from the brow.

Until an uncle chooses to eat paws and snout
before waking each morning, humility in shiny shoes
stalks and rampages a neighborhood.

Sci-Fi Ambience

To prolong sleep for the lullaby
audience that tosses between awareness
and denial, parents replace
security blankets with mentors
and practical goals. Tucked in snug,
mom and dad ride the planet with a snore
if the totems continue to hold tight.
Without question, generations age
and wish not to be disturbed,
button-down to assurance,
but greater infestation claims the terrain.
Honoring death by dozing all day,
the fetish followers recite
the only way in the world: Zzz.
A responsible party seems not to exist:
Cranked music late and fingers pointing
pop on both sides. Bodies without faith
in human resource excommunicate
the zealot from bricks and muscle.
Dormant populations reproduce:
Creed creatures multiply and memorize
$$$ with flash drive and shortcuts.
Struggle loses definition, becomes flabby,
and selves never get worked out.

"Welcome Mat!"

What falls from the animal kingdom
tumbles into selfhood and language
weeping among the flora: feeding fatsia.
Even a dog on a leash and a vegetable
garden inspires kicking a stone.
A tendril lash holds a tear
for movers and shakers. The preyer
and preyed soup-line blister
with picnic frenzy and prove
to inflict supernatural pain. But the trip
from banana skin to this poem packs
no pajamas with a ho-ho joke
that then slaps (with a long handle)
a bruise on a smile. Fingers pinch
an inch to test the container, who
with ink and voice attempts to mimic
the experience that sloshes around
among veins, tendons, and tendencies:
Impression nine, take two.
The bucket and noises may pull
on sleeves, but only to show
a frown and the down-at-the-mouth
that another breath provokes.
The punching bag loves with sonnets
the pounding that the heart can provide.

Silver Platters

Lowering the mirror so eyes engage
with the world that steadies a head
to sites, the age explorer saves
a life from the well. The pupils
teach the senses by example.
Marco Polo studies longitude
and latitude to investigate the space
between first breath and death.
Magellan reports the seasons
in reason on a watermelon.
Neil Armstrong embraces
a moment alone and takes
a step to insure never to return.
The waiter on the long opportunity
holds a tray for the 80-year feast—
if the hunger paces the courses.
All the while feet tap and fingers drum,
gaping out from a cistern,
a reflection known as Solipsist
swallows lifetimes by the town.

Protocol for a Parable

People lay in a box for burial, a science
that doesn't respond. The practical
questions pronounce and perform rites.

Mystic-eyed folk attempt ear to mouth
resuscitation of the corpus, but facts
overwhelm the myth muscle
and rigor mortis parts bad breath.

Pallbearers tug the tub sloshing
imagination and politics to a hole
where granite grows impatient.

A supernaturalist writes up
a lab report and reads it to survivors
who cannot believe.

The family who can't go home
goes to work pretending
last year throws light tomorrow.
Wild flowers visit earth around stone
where schoolchildren narrate beginnings.

The reflexes discovered by
curious and desperate populations
produce wiry hypothesis and thumbnail
theory. Though faith in computing
has dragged brutality along with it,

knowledge razzes uneven
parallel bars and obstacle
courses to save the night out for young
and old. Half-measures interrogate
any dancing upon cemetery lawn.

The Banality Drama

During the catastrophe, the chorus
members rehearse until, but not for, death.
Lead victims may fix to a smile in the end
while collateral damage continues to cry.

By attending to acting lessons,
the cast imitates while masking
against children choosing uniforms in public.
The shrinking prison pants at the prospect.

When close enough to perfect,
the discipline dandy streets credibility.
Mere intimation opens for the fraud
who owns, worships, and rests on morale.

The jobber patches for need,
points toward idols and adapts to hobbies:
The authentic nobody tags dangle,
unprized from around the noosed necks.

Names seem to hold the singers decaying
among dogs and cats in the alley.
Ground between Earth and moon, the stars
at every stage fold over in character, Tada:

At the catastrophe theater banality plays at now.

Hero

Shaken and stirred,
the jarred biochemical
endangers for a lifetime
if sitting on a shelf.

The mixture
between trauma and desire
threatens to detonate
the bottled up orphan
and the lost-to-duty anima.

Action figures and stands
to multiply tricks times gadgets
so a secret secretes into code:
How does freedom mean
while the footed force forms?

The psyche with limbs
holstered just incase

stays tuned.

Tools

"Anxiety is the dizziness of freedom."
—Kierkegaard

Cranium Terrarium

Spelunkers rappel into wells to splash around in mine reflections. Many would not enter the mind at all if it were not for the adrenaline rush in the appearance of such a large number of family resemblances everywhere eyes were cast, the self-absorbed bungee jumpers leaping into spongy mirrors. However, the glint of roles and possibility energize the species attached to vines and lines. Within each cave, weasels do the dirty work for glands and organs that pull on their tails. With so many phantoms and shady underworld characters the umbilical cord thug pulls organs together while believing it controls its mother. An orchestra of Tommy guns performs its opera. A hardhat re-enters the scene of the primal scream. One headlamp elbows the pitch shadows aside to frame a seer. The torch bearer shuttles a spark in from the eyes and ears in attempts to create a brilliant grotto. The best that any body can do is to reach a teacher into the crevices and drag the stubborn numb lulls into the light of day one at a time until the definition of steward brings action.

Outside, the human mound bulges with limpid brow and prowess. Other swells parting eyelids crawl into their own holes for similar reasons, but each alpha animal assures itself that the landscape can only study and stare at one particular lump of ligaments and lipids. Meanwhile the mountain and valley grow tiered and tired, and the sea empties and swills. Even the cold poles tip their caps to water. Trees don't hold their ground. A flea ranges the endangered caged bear.

Cave Dwelling

Daily, any tears not used
to scrub the floors well in eyes
to instruct footing for tomorrow.

The buckets lent for consolation leak,
weeping: dew better, dew better.

The choreography between trauma
and a smile twists and shouts,
so that a vision unrocked and unshamed
by back drop never arrives in dreams.

Too many forks in the road determined
after the starting point and muddle
for imagining a hard right or left.

Now, good intentions carry for the dead end.

Here, invisible to citizens not banished
by Plato, long divergent paths craft
while machines mine with information
for the philosopher kink:
Exhausted will consumes.

Hypnopompia

During the unconnected moment
when darkness lets go and thought
breaks the horizon, a rocket ship
could not bridge the distance
between any sense and objects
outside skin. The costume and role
need nothing from the embedded body.
The rays from passion define the world
and engagement embraces blank sheets.
Waiting for feet to be thrown
from the bed to certainty, emotion
scorches every muscle behind lids
and marches from cranium to toes
carrying bones for torches to rouse
farmer and slicker to arms and legs.
Desire rages, turning to ash
undeserving neighborhoods
along the way. (Compromise
hasn't been invented: The butt
for the mid-day jokes can walk
onto the movie set with a grin.)
Once a sole human hits the floor,
sublimation fleshes out the details
with thumb whorls and taste buds.

Hypnagogia

When the head looks behind
to rest, accomplishment
or achievement feathers
falling asleep. Any semiconscious
compositions paste hope
to the forehead for the morning
mirror. Atlas can encourage
progress enough to a point
to ignore the critic and villain
entering the room at night.
An effort that exhausts muscles
also weights brows and weakens
lids open for business so
that the skull could sleep
on a curbstone: An emergency
exit padlocked. Ditch diggers
rejected the shovel-leaner long ago.
However, a half-baked idea
or a loafer in the garden
for an hour ensures insomnia:
The prince suffers a pea
when in the soup on a mattress.
The ceiling cursor winks word-ready.

Ethic Op Props

The Moses for birthdays on all fours
poses with populations one at a time
saddled on his back. But the elephants
with tykes at the helms determine adult behavior.
So few go right after the memorization and drilling.

Yikes! Harnesses around fat lies and jungle laws
fit bits into the peanut breath explaining the universe.
G-o-o-d: whatever a person does: just.
Left to Paradiso, a road for trained horse-trains
goes through the hearts owned
by potential newspaper subscribers.

The dizzy plot to surprise their lot,
put away violins and pull out machine guns.
The most advanced cheek/cheek nations
water board their way along the golden rule.
Kids squat in the dirt playing eyeballs and teeth.

Virtuous crests carry virgins to the victors.
Faulty folk figure out the huge grey areas
that condemn them to death by trunks:
self-deception convinces friend, family, communities.

Take the two tablets before bedtime:
wherever the aught, guilt sings a lullaby alibi.
Perched on a hot air balloon, even mother doesn't escape
dilemmas, consequence, and grand piano excuses:
one more saint with a riding whip
splashing around a gene pool.

At the thunderous foot, the Thou Shalt Not puzzle
somehow survives rainy days, though empathy scurries

away from the brush. Accident has it one by fun,
the charms that distract evil for better
crimp under the weight waiting for opportunity.

Geologist Pick

Panning sentences for consciousness,
the counter-intuitive prospector
along intelligent life puts to use
precious mettle in a sieve.
Each scoop for orienting
nouns, verbs, the genuine articles
hopes to add to the semiotics
associated with one necklace
and another: Good news muse reply.
Though many gallons
from qualified authors
flow past the rocks soothing ledges,
most sleuth sluices amount to mud
slapping against poetic sensibility.
Clichés, some with platitudes
and deep protocol walls,
rub in gritty sequins that act and act.
Lump-times though the dirt pays:
intimating laundry in a line.
With a sock half full, an exclaimer
limps up a bank and at the jeweler bench
loops eloquent wealth
that sparkles further response.

Whinny Wear

Broken at first breath
and at every step along the way,
the body leashed to the brain
buckles against initiation.
Preparation for death ropes
and saddles for a horse
that hopes for stirrups too.

Nature / nurture compete
to snap any innocent stretch.
Yogi sins bury in mantra: Lasso yahoo.
Bent, folded, mutilated,
not long after delivery an athlete
beats on goal posts in frustration
as a record slips by the tears.

The crumbling woman with a cane
defies when moving across a room
to watch a burgeoning branch;
each exhale extends for the bough,
the shoot, and the bud before the bloom.

The Infiltrated State

"a garrison in a conquered city"
—Freud

Under siege for a hundred years,
the resident at Ft. Psyche,
knees to chin against an archway,
pinches a leg or cheek to prove
consciousness owns a lid or two.
Colonizers landed on the assured
countenance and independent id
and dug in for the fright:
a pox on all the guts.

With spectacle and fanfare,
the march for dimes swarmed
the cities to build character.
Marketing champagne rallies
hurled distraction into dreams
and with intoxicants punched holes
into the bulwark round play.

The secretary for the interior
dangles by the staple that sanity requires,
a post-it-note for effigy seekers.
Mr. and Mrs. Lego find paradise
in the slave-to-debt department.

Staring back at whoever looks up,
the big eye bought the sun and moon that swing
in the sky, and from 'toons to doom
occupies the regions around each thought.
Well intentioned allies and partisans

in the sewers and in the attics give away
the store and address a Russian doll via satire.

Governing platitudes and treads
elevate trances to calm nerves
with opportunities to experience
through sit-coms and video games,
the empathy and envy bungee cords.
The surgical strikes against
the pneuma to drag Élan Vital
through the streets for stoning,
and the yoke, deprive bliss and will.

Anatomic Passion

The epidermis protects against pestilence
and petulance so abstract thought
and lame ideas show up with some definition,
a muscle for a tattoo for mom.
Even a spinal column appears
on a blank sheet to build scaffolding
for nursing flabby images
that embarrass any dwelling.

However, sometimes a dim wit admits to a mitt
or fist folder where a glove with fingers fits.
Pockets fill with prosy notions
that slosh from coast to boast.
Pouches for new born inklings hop
on one leg and then a second until the last.

When breathing punctuates under skin,
the alpha letters form around the aura
until flesh bristles into a hump
and stands with full attention:
Eyes printed on a tongue.

Common Senses

The rods and cones
that distinguish and describe suffer.
Dog whistles winging around the retina
bark and disrupt during observation.
Blind spots misdirect on tongues
when savoring a solution.
Callouses stink with each
touching moment.
The landscape exhibits for living
among haphazard senses too busy
blossoming or shutting down.
The raw material begs
for enhancers, sensors, apps,
but machines that compute
commune with tambourines also.
Every state minds to enforce states
while private thoughts and possibility,
clutching derelicts, exit
through windows in dire escapes.

Dear Great Grandchildren,

A guide led the group of fact finders and truth seekers away from a cave's large mouth through his purgatorial categories toward Darwinian unassuming paradise. For the first two legs of the journey, the hunter and gather dragged information with knuckles, behind, and did so quietly and in fear, we like to imagine. To this day, new information becomes history overnight. When the dark corners of homes were left for good and evil, and fantasies of grottos, catacombs, and hell carried torches well into yesterday, allegories lit up the evening sky. One nearly carried half the globe to some forbidden city in the heavens of absolute zero.

At the half-way house, the addicts wouldn't take off their diapers. At first, monkeys laughed at the feces theses, but when the adult bags of wind mapped out the family trees, reservations became more patient with urges to nail things down. Before the moon became a plum on the ends of thumbs and monkeys, fish, and amoebae were elevated to god status, beliefs asserted themselves with penises and other tools. Censuses, after birthrates and death counts, determined who stood and who prostrated. The armies of men charged each other and then charged the women in thinking through what would be honest and credible.

It took what seemed millennia to get the spotlight off the dark side's Ben Herr and Bend Her sets. The waves of trauma continue to rock the solar system ship, making many passages sick. Today, another day as parasites and so leeches continue to pig pile on the oldest books to make literal news while sucking on the cavern airs of the mine mine. The old hardheaded living quarters own easiest access, and the taboo of any work that doesn't require repeated motor skills fastens its tentacles to fingertips. The binary entrails tail us out of the stalls and into the public arenas. After the last period is a good place to start your marks.

Yours, now, Truly Guilty also.

Fiction Friction

Resting a head on doubt
clears the primrose and wall flower
from the dance hall.
Daisy and Iris rock
with Bud and Timothy.
A humming generator
provides the music.
The charge, distrust, piques
and zaps breathing with creativity.
Sleep idles halfway,
pinching dreams into images.
Feet to perspectives meet the beat
or would get shot by the Wild West
cliché in the saloon.
The electricity in the moment
stabilizes in every whether,
the neither here nor there,
and nerve takes root.
While the courage to nap
powers participation,
the two step scorches continents.

Argh and then Argot and Matey

Jolly parrots command the ship.
Laughter steers starboard
while orgasm leans leeward.
It won't be said again.
The first articulation
may have been the wind
in May and thus Gus the sail,
or a tree in a forest.
No telling from anywhere else.
Certain that a captain
would be serious,
ventriloquists mock
to avoid or garner punch lines that smart.
The bag of wind with a goatee,
Greek oar, and/or an old chestnut
for a hook must have made
a big bang out of space.
Roger wants a cracker,
meat on bones but continues
his fast fingers crossed.
The prisoners stick out
their chests and act brave,
but a quack and buck with ears
push the poet off the diving board.
Oops. The waves bring near
the cheer in the splash. Bye, bye.

Speech Act Moment

With generations to go before arrival
at the stone for touching, the couplings
on the train waste phony places on fingerprints:
mourning caresses sprinkle holy time pieces
in the soon garden where only a poem grows.
Too immature to handle, the unfit perspectives
work the kaleidoscope and die old,
marking time. The air-condition prepare-men
boss meteorologists, landscapers,
interior designers, and gurus
so that every excuse circulates in copper tubing
or jettisons into outer space.
Anticipating the honest day when
cages never close and lovers and loners
think on the house, workaholics
lay down bottlenecks, traffic jams,
and their lives. Great grand children
may then frolic in the accurate sentence
served by mountains of bone.

Ouch, All Together

Misery loves symphony. Violence
giving tympani. Too bad. Cat gut
everywhere. Bows and bows.
Witnesses oboed out of the way.
Suck it up on a harmonica.
Better yet use the bad breath
and exhale irony. The hand
contorted and expensive material.
The hand-contorted and expensive
material. The hand contorted
and expensive material.
When three quick-witted
conversationalists with symbols.
Musketeers crashing rabbit ears
for each other live.
The piercing champagne
is how anyone knows where
to put fingers. Welcome
orphan unity to join in.
Fog horns poke ivory around
for the vulnerable playing.
The islands forcing silence
on lips camouflage unnatural acts:
a snicker, a laugh.
Feathers run-ith over with flutes.
Now is talking.
Wee jumps in
anytime 3/4. Or else.

Dogged

Scratching accusations,
chasing empty promises
into lakes, and on hind limbs
nipping at paychecks,
domesticated workers feed
at impossible pacts,
any solidarity. Animus heels
to the mite in any attack
and the self-conscious itch focuses:
The bone hauls sharper teeth home.
At the foyers the important guests
welcome the fetch and news.
The four-legged human lifts a paw
and waters sod that patches pride.
The moon sleeps through
the evening performances at every
fenced-in lawn and backdoor.
On a short leash, the best friends
to industry put their snouts
to grind stones for sons and daughters.
If the scent permits,
the K-9s follow a meat grinder;
if let loose, the hounds whimper.

Asteroid Nations

Small worlds last longer
on the green felt table
than Jupiter or galactic thought
imagine. Graveyard pockets
swallow giant globs also;
even the cued run risks
following conductor batons.
The phalanx against the odds
and accuracy protects eight balls
frightened in consequence.
The big shot elite crack
into each other producing points
to remember for pop quizzes,
and grand designs.
The cosmopolitan sojourner
owns homes in multiple city outskirts
and blows smoke over the gin,
but neighborhood solitaire
by wrinkled women wager
and wink another day.
The minor constellation
each generation propels enshrines
the passing star, an oblivious entourage
surviving the more meaningful
few cultural existences.

Banality Bulbs

Once the kitchen light has illuminated
the bed, bath, and the women and children
dumped into a mass grave, the sleepwalker
may continue to bathe in screened newspaper
each morning on the commuter rail.
The all-purpose bulbs scrub irises
and grow into sight in the dark.
The sex on a mattress without sheets
but with lips, cheeks, and genitalia
comes out dish water and smeared Formica.
The bottom and shaved stink
flushes for florescence and a spoon.
Noses, limbs, and lime perform act one
in a family-rated musical.
The peaks in orgasm and murder
valley flatten to butcher board
for the dreaming between work and home.
With a banana from breakfast in a bag
Mr. Z walks in shoes already massacred.

The Fix

Every sunrise repair men and women
wielding tool boxes and power cords
enter unhappiness. Wrenches and hammering
pass time with only wise cracks and tease
in the race toward the cemetery sleep.
A momentary illusion for one pleases
the jerry-rigger whose dirty hands shake
with ignorance to maintain a grip
on hope when tweaking the volume
on the background wail. Slapping spackle
and paint upon the faces that cities present
with pursed lips, insuring contentment
suspect, tempers a mad dash to disguise
a smiley face lurking in gentrification.
Nor can a demolition team turn a frown
upside down. The state, Persistent Sacrifice,
just may rid colons from the body politic
only to arrest and throw broken toys
into parentheses for twenty-five years to life.
Exiting exhausted at bedtime, the crew leans morale
against a wall and sheds any twinkle in a corner.

Marshland Rag

In the quagmire the two-step
and marching in place
substitute for moving forward.

However, yielding to the swamp
grows mold, moss, camouflage
around eyes and on rears.

Liver and vessels become muck.
Every body part yearns for mud.

The frog on the lily pad
squatting in the chest
would learn to sing if limbs
weren't bogged down in doubt.

Lifeboat

The long-steamed habits and rituals
kiss at the bow and stern
and with mythology fasten
lengthwise and at ribs.
Without sail, rudder, or oar
marriage lunched when launched.

Calm, waterspouts, and hurricane gale
engage without concern for invention,
ceremony, or flotsam amid currents.
Adrift without spar and soon
without sextant, a compass mock-salutes.

Crest-fallen and heaved, the hull
hollers and gurgles so that
few couples arrive at wherever,
and sometimes one bails against resentment
to harbor for the drowned.

Make believe and half truths
hold for the hold by two.
Boat building teammates
begin with clouds and talk
about fair whether in the drink
or down the sink in a future:
Frantic waves at the passing
once upon a time.

The Catch

"Ruling a large state is like cooking a small fish"
—Tao Te Ching

Cooking a small fish over
three leaping cats with tongues
that hiss at the frying pan brings
minutia in contingency to scales.
Remaining conscious while
the earth moves beneath feet
demands that a hand roasts.
Learned early, the spices dusted
over the muscle, fins, and detail
nets the best taste possible
given flesh dead and alive.
Singed and singing, the bass
in the marinade reels with
a spatula whenever rhythm
provides motive and weight.
The heat in everyday surprises
twists any cold-blooded
slalom run into childhood
memorization. The line taut
with decapitation and gutting
breaks for enjambment and flares
from game oil. Baited parents
put a pout into the pond for
anyone evolved in hip boots
to land for a smile.

The Stash

"[Habit] is the enormous flywheel of society, its most precious conservative agent. It alone is what keeps us all within the bounds of ordinance and saves the children of fortune from the envious uprisings of the poor."

—WILLIAM JAMES

Slug Mug

What matter poses in a cranium
upon Doric and Ionic pedestals
that clutch microchips for hands?
Coincidence, blind spots, and denial
permit the lizard brain access
to the costumes while onstage.
Flesh coats consistency with a riddle.
The camouflaged armor swallows
the matter and weaponry nose to nose
and stops with diversion
the speaking throat.
In victory on Greek and Roman
shoulders, epochs permit
the salamander to recognize
with empathy the hunger
and self-defense in everything
physical in the air and in the dirt.
On the leather heals during
Masterpiece Theatre,
T-Rex sheds light but left skin
with the contagion that peopled
every locality. A snail solidarity
blazes a revolutionary tale.
From hemisphere to hemisphere
the croc continues with nails
and scales behind eyes
and smiles that fit heads.
A tongue dices an entire audience.

That Mean Mirth

The bridges over schadenfreude
collapse into the joy.
A catastrophe somewhere else
saves another day.
The animal won't be avoided.
Hyenas bare the shadow at colleagues.
The fjords grit and hold breath.

Phew and wiped brow
get empathizers through to charity,
the best for which a tunnel can hope.
Pity throws an arm around shoulders,
a friend while dividing the loot
from the conquered.

Libraries, galleries, concert halls,
and theaters fill the hungry neighbor
with characters and circumstances,
confusing a juggler with files to finger tips,
allowing a victim to escape perhaps.

But enough craft can wake
fellow flesh to the skin
not yet stretched on the floor
or hung on a wall.

Dressing Despair

A mirror stands among the cynics
who fix ties and skirt issues.
Side show poems distort
when fog or thought shards threaten.

What seems convex or concave
details for full-length humans:
Graying hair, stain-spotted shirt,
scuffed shoe, seams.

Best to sign up for what
doesn't need addressing,
join broken extended families.
Sour the "well" from which
the honest guy or gal draws water.

So while the quiet and inactive
clothing hanging around suits
for an era, the overwhelming might
turned inward enough to style,
to focus attention.

With no time, no courage
to reflect on words
the sidewalk crowd forms
into a gang behind the bully,
remains in the school yard
another decade.

In the Morass

With a start beneath two brows,
the digestive tract sucks up
to the low hanging fruit
(Venus, Mars) while rumbling
through desire spitting pits
and dumping dreams behind.
The essential prune
for the paradise and host toast.
When lips part to coax
and the esophagus stretches
a neck, intestines prepare for
determination and advertises
a place to park natural resources
. . . forever: Yoga mogul.
Worming a way through
everything outside the human body,
wit hands off the idea
to cold calculators.
Tick workers dismantle
and build to spec monstrosities
in a belly, Humvees strip-teased
into plows and addressed again
vice with verse. Never satiated,
the python continues to spy,
to conjure, to swallow and to parse
for use. Use: Practical applications
and a narrow marrow in breath.

Milk in the Newspapers

The illusion holding up pants
exposes itself to the waist
and doesn't buckle under
counter-argument eyes.
The little emperor has polished floors
with a trouser accordion for years.
Luck had it that official offices
and buses never had to be run for.
Everyone, going about business
along the daily parade route,
smiles and waves. The weather vane,
crafted from crotch and butt,
reassures with misinformation.
After all, how many pants huff
until the opportunity to net
a big boy draws a lot?
Not by the way any longer,
even women own two legs
and enough imagination
to pleat a skirt and show off
an exasperated thigh.
Public blind spots treat
noise makers the same given chance.
So sometimes musicians
wear top hats and white gloves only.

Neighbor Relations

Catching a sunny shade of flush,
each pouch of air greets a palm,
while whistling into oblivion.
The flocks of angels compose
the floating wool of skies
at the cemetery's prize.

Iris for cornea, the poke
of revenge exacts its violence
for beings alive: politics over heaven.
The blind party of thumbs punch
and hors d'oeuvres of deception
wrestle into grounds.

The diplomat of preemptive strikes
grabs attention of foe to farm
using foreign toil and soil.
The only hell singeing waits on
the taste buds of the victor—
over easy or shoe leather kisser.

Modern Justice

Empathy provides users shoes
and leather gloves; wishful thinking
sops up tears. The moralist
walks a mile in the cold
with extremities intact.

Once inside a house the puppet master
imitates walls but warms cockles
with vocal cord chords,
and can't help twitching fingers.

Experience requires infinite lifetimes,
while determined accuracy
and desperate people remain poor.
Novels absorb the readers
and let the victims down.

The addicts roam the streets
to slip a hand to empty coffee cups
and soon after in lazy boys
fix eyes with cable syringes.

Fabric Fault

The buttons for shame
sewn by parents and teachers
fasten shirts, blouses, and pants;
so disappearing acts
take place for lifetimes.
The zip from guilt to second try
seems silk for the quick-change
artist pleated to better behavior,
but not for a named "bone-exposed,"
pinned from lapels, humiliated
into rage or ghost. Forgiving
the mirror for the wound
that needs a wink to cure, brings
friends and family to stitches
in no time. The same error blamed
on the core dares a threat
to violence an absence to breathe.

Diatribal Tangent

Emerging from the root cellar
most skaters wear hip boots
and carry carving knives.
Wild animals and weed seeds
scatter from the dinosaur revival site.
History books slosh over waist bands
and soak the heavy pants
with every surgical move by ballerinas.
Bibles bubble up.
The etymological flower child
loses its way and fondles tub and mud.
Slipping across mushroomed floors
and plunging through glass
water tables in cold weather,
fallen fruit insists on understanding everything
while the stars adjust their lenses
and the monad yawns. The evidence
poured a concrete foundation
that reigns from every tendril.
So the constant reminding and gratitude
seems to plead for a frozen lake. Questions
swallow hard without room for shovels
at their moment. The potatoes and carrots
ground the compass into black pepper.
The core in the Earth rots for mayors and miners
to make with top soil and crust.
The watch towers spray anything germinating
with caution and send protesters
to strike with limbo bars:
cow turds for Martians.
With a prune beneath all sleep,
the toddler salvaging the lumber
from a nursing home shuffle

won't save survival for its key.
A titmouse poses a canary inquest,
while the gas works
threatens bedfellow universities.
In every sigh from boredom,
in each privileged pronunciation,
a sprig from below sucks on the life
from around it. Top toil could remember that.

Cities' Limits

Faith in death frees the worshipper
from consequence and result. Atheists
dance with rabbits feet and patches,
extending joyful relics ad nauseam.
Monks slobber around China, bumping
against one end of broad daylight
to the other, letting chain reactions
chug at the ends of their lines.
Cradle / grave
Cradle / grave
Cradle / grave
paved in zs,
while revelers avoid cats,
ladders, and mirrors.
Writing the trains every day,
the far out parishioners don't hide
in suburban homes where
the radio blares
Womb to womb
Doom the tomb
Womb to womb.
From the heart of the city,
Ain't Saint replies "Bless me less me
because I sin."

The Prime Prevention

Should these body parts
or those body parts enter
the room, every living thing
near should shudder. Instead,
the candy-coated subconscious
masks and props as though habit
doesn't crack without pressure
or melt under a sunny day.
The tall totems and bulldog taboos,
the conventions and protocols,
and the elongated work ethic
all busy and steer many neighbors
into depositing shares
into the Good Will boxes.
But then expectation closes eyes,
so when the love turns sour
or the resentment overflows
the banks and police departments,
cities go into shock.
The shaken pleasure principals
then need to unlearn the explosives
contained as guts or organs
so the Darwin family can slip
into something more comfortable.

Tongues

When talking with the I'd,
harmony needs more
than its orchestral instruments.
Squiggles that remind organs
around a skeleton that periods
have sentences don't add up yet.
How sweet that dance and song
get along so well. Who knows what
may be driving the shadow caster.
The parasite that doesn't understand words
owns metaphors and similar
devices by another frame.
Any bridge comes from a top hat
at a magic show and stretches
until it disappears. Irony
must also signal out across
the unthinkable. A baboon bassoon
may jog memory but breaks wind
for desire deeper than chapped skin.
Perhaps marriage counseling
would help inspire conversation
to prevent the hand in glove from
the candy store and more.
Ten-foot poles poke distances to divide
an otherwise day for mayhem.
Many folks pick one up on the way
through childhood or sooner.
However, two tin cans and a string
would bring a universal language
to mediation and crossing a ponder.

Game

Before flopping
into an over-stuffed easy chair
the tongue takes aim
at barn doors and with buckets
and broom-sized strokes
slaps on a coat.

Dabs glob
and drip.

No representational artist
with twisted tubes,
a palette, and beret
cocks within ear shot.
Even a sash brush sasses
as on a hog.

Senses surround
before the taste buddy wags, so
excess and history scrub
against each utter worded:
A lie lays on the canvas, victor.

The deer escapes,
but the outdoors, the hunt:
Over there, did a branch move?

Twenty-four Hours News Channel

Funneling world crises
through a keyhole, cameras
and microphones aim to drench
with caring, the bigot with a spigot.
The tears from all corners in hell
rust cities in peace, but the pupil
in one room for living
governs the leaky faucet.
The smell from dead flesh
wafts at least a continent
away as the odor from local
squatters fills police noses.
Any scratching at the door
doesn't reach the ears inside,
so entertainment surrounds
frowns on a couch.
Before a bed no prayer needs to prop
a wall in pieces and unhinged.
Strangers knock yet,
and a splinter embeds muttered storms.

The Surprise Parties

The unbidden, with its optional oxygen
penetrating lungs and pores surrounds
the population, whether city or country,
complies with the standards of homeland security.
Storefronts' attempts to distract disasters
and diversion with bargains galore
from the locked and alarmed backdoor fail,
bankrupting the compulsive closet organizer.
Battering rams, hairpins, and the frontal assault
of old women with large purses flooding
the undergarment department may muddy
the owner's books with red ink.
Or the whole street may in its slow turn
go out of fashion. No accounting
rationalizes the undesirable facts
from any scene lived by anyone.
Would-be surrealist painters found themselves
in a corner when brushed against the terrorist.
Houdini couldn't tell who dun it
during his last trick. If mind-gamers couldn't
keep the hound from the boar,
what makes the petty boo voila see
a different mate? The master of many guys is
and will catch up with hare and owl,
a little today and with plots tomorrow.
However here today, crazy frequenters
to the bazaar celebrate the birthdays
of those jacks-in-boxes who don't jump out
of their skins, but rollup their sleeves
and unbutton the necks of their shirts.

Habitual Habitat

Intuition sops up tenderness,
tension, trauma, and anything else
around a body with the mop.
The grunge sponge hints
and suggests for influence and rot.

Any fig leaf that demands attention
for wringing and arranging signals
into data deserves suspicion;
so the foliage suggests.

And a mirror reveals that moments
steal articles and verbs and subjects
from vegetation uprooted.
Regardless, the hide can't be hidden.

The flabby apps seem to cover
the subconscious, muscle mass,
and hexed organs, but the background
seam grips the sense center
between teeth in a smile.

Story Lines

The terms, negotiated by heart beats
or freak accidents, or the hand
that signs no contract,
inhibit the lexicon inhabited, owned.
The shorter sentences, thought
to have garnered clemency
from the inevitable, fill with second best,
consolation, and grand
eyes friends wear for any occasion.
Longer strings in exclamation
or depression clip productivity
at its knots and motives.
Multiple chapters burn a lover
with look-alikes or drag a victim
who refuses to try. However,
the corporeal desires to write
the end screen all breezes past
alphabetical orders.

Behind the Lines

Stories camouflage authenticity from the teller.
Native narratives, woven to the left and right,
shade eyes; intentions grow invisible
around tall tales. Stones for glass houses
color the aim in confessions.
An epic blends city buildings, wit, crowds.
Accidental audiences hear a harp chord
in passing or deliberations concentrate,
but the listener also yammers on
arriving closer and closer to conviction,
a home fire with a hassock.
Empathy recognizes squirming
when changing position in a chair.
Defoliation ears or quakes that move
each person from cornerstone alibis
develop empty promise for the refrain,
and ballad time germinates lush
brushes with sprites and spites.
And so the dress-up party clothes
to wait for the hunter to duck.

Denial Bile

Sprezzatura grabs neighborhoods by their throats.
Even grandmothers conceal their weapons in public.
Gangsters practice yoga breaths to keep
from swearing with right hands-on Bibles.
Children study cool weather on their ways
through the parks to school.
Armies at ease shop at homes and return home.
The virtue that coats the town in red
and doesn't set in the evening inspires
a whole people. Earth swallows
a population. Oceans gut ships.
The sky falls around chins
suffocating tall living. Still,
the commuter rail drags more bodies
to the sacrifice. The icing
at the centers, while the news spreads
and hyper-extends core chores,
collects political figurines from admiration.
Each personal disaster drips magma down
calm concrete canyons that buzz with honeybees.
Rumor has it that cold mash potato mounds
threaten the newcomers even while the Sphinx
nibbles at hors d'oeuvres leading each line.
__ and the word steak passes from lips
in chain reaction. The calamity press
that starches pants from lungs increases
the perfect hair. During the matches
and steamed mob, no sweat.

In Skin Sin

Dripping into need, empathy drags January.
Intravenous pities patients. Sufferers
beg the cold, sweat small stuff.
Molasses competes in kindness. Sweet
revenge grips handouts in quiet.
The gravity in riverbeds denies oil
upward mobility so spare change
or peasant uprisings begin
with sympathy on mountain tops.
When blind roam streets,
the sleeping lob peaks, a coincidence
until the fun wears holes in sheets.
If money bags spring a leak
or lose a limb, a Bleak Corps
member bleeds for the Red Cross,
but leech encrusted bodies
seep post and beam.
Privileged palm whorls may care to dip
a toe (wade around) in clod-hoppers.
The callused hoof buckles
up under its freight.

For the Ride

Death drives the vehicles in chests.
The bad boy cruises around town
upsetting fruit carts and old women
in babushkas. Americans
don't believe in Santa Claus,
but brats always welcome toys.
Unlimited sales kills joys
in want, desire tires, deflates.
Pinch flesh a little and pleasure
grows an inch. The sadist
paddles behind the scenes.
A tippy canoe, carried a birch
sorority, and Tyler too ended up
with a red bottom. Reverse
goes nowhere, a hammer and sickle
prop pickle. Pedal to the metal
and wee is living. The racing
through to everything loved
doesn't own headlights. Beyond
wheeling everything dust,
the Thunderbird plays chicken
with everyday giving,
cheers the bungee cord jump
in rising each morning,
the scrambling for the dear.

The Drive

Grasping satori at 10 and 2:00
and prepared to stomp on either pedal
while reeling through back streets,
the eternal adolescent anxiety
proves for the mettle jalopy
by guiding passion among potholes
and ditches, past strip clubs
and chapels, circumventing
recruitment stations and retirement ruts.

The author, insisted on
by the fictional character,
learns too well every chip that flies
from the granite block
and every flake that could but doesn't.

To ride the axel and miss the drama,
the walking dead escapes from the journey,
the last man buckles up in enlightenment.

Until the Ferris wheel bucket bottoms out
for the last time the perpetual identity crisis
whitens knuckles for a fortune without cliché,
the monumental grave moment.

Garden Expeditions

"It is a matter of living in that state of the absurd I know on what it is founded, this mind and this world straining against each other without being able to embrace each other."
—Camus

"...to leave / even one's own first name behind, forgetting it / as easily as a child abandons a broken toy."
—Rilke

Isolation Station

The young Prometheus skipped
steps when scaling the pyramid
that holds Maslow. RIP.
After the North-Face-King dance
with purposelessness and the long
laughter for cleverness,
an old goat returned to needs missed
along rough terrain. Mountaineers
camping on a coveted crag
didn't welcome a homecomer
who wished to share space.
Cliff dwellers, jockeying for vantage point
yet intimate with altitudinal nosebleed
cures, routed the seeker who provoked fights
while giving away maps and a used pick ax.
Humiliation returns the brass
figure to the trophy top where liver
welcomes crows, and echoes
course through ravines on all sides.

Home on the Range

The stadium fills each day,
a soup bowl around a crouton.
Sofas surround a woman
wearing a television set
with legs that go on forever
or a computer screen.
Moving in for the slaughter
requires education and resumes.
The spectator at the national
coliseum places thumbs in eyes
to let life drain into a sewer
system for the dynamo.
Almost every chef boils water
to pour a bath. Few ingredients
fall into line for life originale.
Cooking and fermentation time
spoon for the excused absence.
The sip that sits at the edge
for lips mocks iPod, iPad.
A lone stranger rides out
from the sunset once perhaps
in every blue moon. To get
started the inventor needs
to get started: Police barricades
trigger the conviction that nothing
goes on here, move along.

Facing the Many Small Bangs

The freak planet among stars
seemed to require leaning
on crosses and crescents.
Step two left the lame
wielding crutches to maim
swingers with opposing limps
and occasional and avid walkers.
Propping gods by the armpits,
evangelists threaten with club mentality
deviation from rite routines:
Emergency wards surrounded
and flattened dwellings on tomorrow.
Martyred secularists lined the roads
holding olive branches between teeth.
Of course the butchers and bakers
represent clergy using reliable gadgets
to give moms and dads meaning.
But the butchers and bakers
stand in for high-tech innovators also.
Both limb loppers continue
to conduct inquisitions to garner
warriors on knees. Scheherazade,
the cosmic dancer, survives
children denying that the dark owns.

Bungle Bundle

With bones for props,
the sack for sorrow
attempts to isolate within desire
that breaks the horizon with distractions.
The meat within the bag lining
steadies to aim, to swipe at
the low-hanging, the in-the-way,
and look-a-likes
that soon sour into regret.
After noon when intent forgives
and heals for second chance,
another try; needs wobble
under the lugging toward nightfall.
The cinch on the muffled duffel gags
with struggle and strife
before a pillow for the smallest hope
for home town streets
promises to curb a dream
by stuffing a wail with hunger.

Self-Help Medium

A séance channels into a hand
from crevices in writing
that still steals eyeballs somewhere
every evening. Articles keep watch
while nouns and verbs dredge
without a word spoken. Spaces
advise sshh. Blood flows
from a coffin onto a page
and marbles roll into tomorrow.
Once under the influence,
the novelist careens across broad
daylight drunk under the bed sheet
thrown over the costume-partier.
"Boo" becomes the genre when
the cover opens to revelers.
The adult child smiles at bones
arranged until invisible on paper.

Off the Grid

To rewire a brain for interested
dwellers in the West, a hack
from the East pulls exposed cables
and cords from wall outlets
and light fixtures: Ohm. (Lightning,
the key for fearlessness, strikes up
conversations all about kites
but never cracks a downward
facing smile on the frightened.)
Engineers then plan for rut diggers
who feel around the dark searching
for a big switch. With a flick
in wrists palms come together
to honor, without applause,
unseen gods. The sunbird and dog
wait to master the tree rooted
in a meditation on light
to prepare for the oncoming.
The circuits open 24 / 7 can be
counted on one hand clapping.
Groovy folk wish to own the tool
with the holy cow attachment
the way wall street executives
wear golden parachutes.

The Motorway

A fetish alternates between
money and conscience.

The two pistons powering
the internal combustion culture
drive whole classes off the orgasmic end.

The philanthropist yawns
and stretches a philosophy each morning
even while guilt promises more action.

Sex owns little ignition with this fever.
Labor suffers the invisible thumb.

The smooth ride on the single-minded asphalts
opens toll roads toward wealth,
redemption, and the jerk into the deep sleep.

Economists and holy men ratchet up
and apply brakes in the pits on warranties.

Governing bodies kick oil cans
and pump liquidity.

All while a poor bastard in the dust
continues walking toward the excitement.

Moving Fixtures

Ushering other possibilities into oblivion,
the halo around each actor
shows to audience members on stages
a long threshold.
An angel finds no body
but other realities scratch heads.
The dark theater harbors
explanations for what might have been
surprises. Moving lungs if nothing else
along becoming, populations escape
the time-lapse photography,
cling to a cartoon character.
Thom Thumb peeping through blinds
returns home with sexual satisfaction.
The greener grass skirts the longest yard.
And flip through the most boring life
and the sweat and tears
involved in self-assurance
build metropolitan areas.
Jockeys on desire flap bent elbows
around concrete potentials never chased.
Zeitgeists have little to do with the unimagined.
Around the town lay the ruins from
buildings not drawn, never whipped into shape.

Knock Knock

The door-to-door open-mind hello-fan
in wedge-toed, flatiron-soled shoes
with railroad-spiked treads!

The soul-suited intruder in a hat that tips,
could help with grandma crossing the street,
and schoolwork if the teacher thinks about Junior.

A scale readies under hair for weighing
opinions and the onion arguments wrapped in news.

But first, a neighbor must be a dweller
and hear the chimes when rung.
Then an occupant must appear, emerge at the door.

Three stories sail after the greeting
with flights into fantasy step-by-step:
The master-listener follows through the thoughts
and the breeze from over the threshold
until the basement bids.

On cue from a toolbox, an oilcan tongue (vital to ears)
enunciates while not unhinging emotions
but pivoting without complaint past the arch.

Roadmap

Along cultural byways,
landmarks and rest stops
mark the pathology.
Pausing for refreshment
leads to witnessing strangers
gathering intelligence
from the various totems,
markets, and shelters
for the various problems
endemic to the population.
The props distract anxieties
with wisdom and local chains
that comfort with links to the past.
Superiority fills the air
for petri dish and scientist.
Returning to the vehicle
that deposited as though
from another planet, the tourist
travels cool and awake
until the terrain and the ruts,
when sleep resumes
for the anthropologist who
then attends to the shackles
and touchstones
long pushed into place.

Grumble, Grouse, Teehee

On the way to the complaint
department the poet selects
from the suggestion box a party hat,
streamers, and a noise maker
that unrolls to a tickle.
While putting grievance to paper,
smiles slip out every corner
the pen takes. The legs under
the desk quiver with excitement,
the four arrows aiming to soar
and make sore. The victim
before the injured proprietor
rests, rests, rests, rests wild, while
limb casts set before an orchestrated
consumer mob at Xmas time.
Hate mail grows. Every article
that the desk carries wags
a finger and the parcels
don't forgive when the simple crashes
and drums roll on the floor.
Only after the storm has lifted
and dust drifts on the last polished
surface do two hands find each other.

Invisible Ink

The poet places one foot and then
another, leaving no impression
on the planet: Any carbon print wears
moccasins over each syllable.
Around the Earth sonnets toddle
donning bonnets for faces that jump
onto buses for work each morning
or slump into a depression that sulks
fully employed. The job dweller
ponders only what stance
would create meals, what boots
will hold the position for tomorrow.
An impractical ghost can sink soles
into farmland and muck up townhouse
carpeting and not a sole in cities
would notice a tread. Though no promises
for utopia pass lips or smudge the page,
the widget for no purpose does
choreograph a way through life
that welcomes stumblers into font
into sound into the dance.

History's Empty Nursery

Every once in nine so oftens
a possible world is glimpsed
from heads pregnant to bursting
with market forces. Gad Zeus Almost!
The passions of technology
and greed conceive an illusion
of Now Bones Stock Exchange
and systemic shifts from brand news.

From cervixes of an ear or mouth
an alien reality crowns as though
everyone's birth were imminent.
Strangers looking for autographs
claim to be relative. Millions
of people wish to gather to stay
in touch. Three kings travel so far.

Unrecognizable, Time Square's party
mask fastens tons of confetti
into dermatology's phonebook.
Then the royal babes of bitches
duck back into the city planners' wombs
from the seduction of pickpockets.
Hawkers surge and swarm
would-be mothers senseless.

Sewing Machine

Time stitches contingencies
into patchwork until history
warms hometowns enough
for sleep. At each intersection
among segments a button reminds.
The unlicensed citizen attempts
to pull vignettes up over the head.
Nightmare spills into the streets
if granny with her pins
and needles waits long enough.
The tossing and learning
on the edge that weaves
now heaves panic to varying
degrees at arrogant survivalists
in full march. Puffed plans
and unmet destinies stuff
each scrap seconds lend.
Some seamstresses and tailors
prefer death day and night.
Other threadbare shiverers
can't close eyes or numb to guilt.
Yarn yawners need
the entertainment industry
to cover the news that props
a pillow to a tickle. However,
tucked in a trunk the old quilt
exposes remnant memory
to feet and wardrobe
for penetrating moments.

On Deck

Visits to the hospital burst
across the bow knocking jib
from mast until the torso
leaks spirit into a nursing home.
Are dinghy and now-not-so yacht
ready for the gurney slide
and christening? Death plays pirate,
forcing captain to tread water
in a diaper. A doctor enters
waving a sword. Pablum providers
swing on the yardarms.
The corked Champaign in ribbon
finery ages still to bat a ball
over the Green Monster
and into a cemetery. S.S. Eulogy
frigate frets. The old fool
weathered strife on the long slip
into home port under dark.
Fair thee well mate!

Fair Thee Well

Whether hunting parties hound
or drones patrol, accidents own
the journey within which homes
stake claims. An alarm clock alerts
Captain Cautious that the mattress
and pillows must go. Manuals
and Youtube videos instruct
proper use, and the A student
follows the prayer to tea.
"Oops" eats lunch, and afternoons
sop caffeine. Even in the evening,
bubble-wrapped Zs saw away
from the inside to meet the dream
in thin air. Driving the car
into the garage or spiking a punch
or basketball in a yard, the miner
strikes rich earth for a pine box.
The goof absorbs brakes, the seat belt,
and air bag just before presenting
impact. Ready Freddy the Eagle Scout
will also lose the pout.

Todestrieb and the Parasite

Around the banquet tables at the cemetery
interest, lust, hunger quit
whether or not balmed daily earlier.

Strutting the latest designs from NASA
and sporting carnival bumpers, desire endures
beyond the havenly, folding body.

The tick-talking retirement party
lunges to catch up
with someone abandoned for forty years.

At the lounge for missing persons
golf club members beat with a driver
and chase with bourbon
to squander regret and redemption.

Stepping over the corpse, the pulp fiction
(a rung, a foothold) cries an infancy
for which cultures scramble with wishes.

The Storage Shed

"I think that means that instead of living under the sun and the moon and the sky and the stars, we're living in a fantasy world of our own making."

—Louis Malle

During the storage shed,
when drafts through the seams
whistle at times, threatening to lift
clay pots from benches, the versed
repair to fix feet to the floor.

Just outside,
      where money reaps
one by one the poor react as predicted
to the assaults so that prison
or the cemetery await;

      where the Palestinian chair,
water board, and sleep deprivation triggers
inducing fantasy for American graduates
from Helplessness High;

      where international schadenfreude
stand guard in the watch towers.

Further outside,
      the spotlight
for the accidental freak show
ignores with mathematical accuracy
allowing the science meme
to talk and walk with arrogance.

Once the contents rest on the curb
with the sign "Free" so to speak only,
two cheeks fill with apple sauce
from a spoon until the clinking
on the bowl falls silent.

www.ingramcontent.com/pod-product-compliance
Lightning Source LLC
Chambersburg PA
CBHW061452040426
42450CB00007B/1327